J
811.008
LAR   Larrick, Nancy

             To the moon and back

To
the
Moon
and
Back

To the Moon and Back

A Collection of Poems
Compiled by
NANCY LARRICK

Illustrated by
CATHARINE O'NEILL

DELACORTE PRESS

Also compiled by Nancy Larrick

PIPING DOWN THE VALLEYS WILD

THE MERRY-GO-ROUND POETRY BOOK

Published by
Delacorte Press
Bantam Doubleday Dell Publishing Group, Inc.
666 Fifth Avenue
New York, New York 10103

The Acknowledgments on pages 81–83 constitute an extension of the copyright page.

Compilation copyright © 1991 by Nancy Larrick
Illustrations copyright © 1991 by Catharine O'Neill

Library of Congress Cataloging in Publication Data
To the moon and back / compiled by Nancy Larrick ; illustrated by
Catharine O'Neill.
    p.   cm.
  Includes bibliographical references.
  Summary : Sixty-six poems by dozens of English and American authors
are full of rhythm and movement and suitable for reading aloud.
  ISBN 0-385-30159-6
  1. Children's poetry, American.   2. Children's poetry, English.
[1. American poetry—Collections.   2. English poetry—Collections.]
I. Larrick, Nancy.   II. O'Neill, Catharine, ill.
PS586.3.T6   1990
811.008′09282—dc20   89-25918
                                                      CIP

Manufactured in the United States of America
March 1991
10 9 8 7 6 5 4 3 2 1
BVG

For Al and Jerian
with my love

Contents

To the Edge of the Dashing Sea

The Jet Stream Roars In

Casting Their Nets for Stars

How Nice to Be a Speckled Frog

Someone Small but a Piece of It All

TO THE MOON AND BACK

Today there is music in the air. Everywhere, from the shopping mall, to the doctor's office, to the ball park. Often we take our music with us all day and then rush home to enjoy the music of radio, TV, and cassettes.

This may be the reason we enjoy the sound of poetry, for poetry, too, has melody. In fact, the earliest poems were meant to be sung or chanted, and many modern poems have been set to music for piano and guitar.

As you listen to a poem being read aloud—and listening is the way to meet a poem, I think—you will feel the rhythm of that poem. It may be the tap, tap, tapping of rain on the roof, the rush and roar of city traffic, or the crooning and mooning of sleepytime. Each poem has its own melody.

Soon you will find that your feelings are drawn into those of the poet. You may be like the girl who said: "I like that poem because it's a little scary." Or because it makes you want to giggle or cry. As one boy put it: "The poet is like me. He feels."

To the Moon and Back is a collection of sixty-six poems that young listeners and readers have enjoyed and asked for again and again. All are full of rhythm and feeling.

Not every poem will be your favorite, of course. As a beginning, you may want to flip through the pages and choose one that seems most promising to you.

Then try reading it aloud—to your friend, to your brother or sister, or just to yourself. When you hear the words—rolling or tripping or swinging along—you will recognize the melody more easily. If you have someone read the poem aloud as you listen, you will hear another voice chanting the same melody in a different way. With a tape recorder, you can listen to your own voice reading the poem. And if you are like me, you will want to make a second or third tape, each time hoping the next one will sound the way the poet intended.

Sometimes it is fun to select a piece of music to play softly as background while you read. It has to provide the right mood for the poem, of course: soft and soothing for "Roll Gently, Old Dump Truck" perhaps, or swinging and swaying for "Multi-Colored Balloon."

Soothing, swinging, scary, happy, sad—whatever your mood, I hope that these poems will lift you right off "to the moon and back."

Nancy Larrick

To
the
Moon
and
Back

*I'll
Tell
You
a
Story*

Hitchhiker

There was a witch who met an owl.
He flew beside her, wing to jowl.

Owl language always pleased the witch:
Her owl at home sat in his niche
And talked a lot about the bats
He met at night, and how the cats
Were scared of him. That sort of thing.
But here was one owl on the wing,
Who said—I don't mean said "Who, Who!"—
Who said, "I've just escaped the zoo.
I'm going home. I haven't flown
Much lately—that is, on my own.
They flew me to the zoo, you know,
Last . . . well, it's several years ago.

"My wings are stiff: I'm tired! *Am* I!
So when I saw you flying by,
I thought 'She's heading north by east.
If I can hitch a ride at least
As far as Pocono, I'll make
It home.' Okay? Is that a rake
Or broom you're flying? Sure! A broom.
I see it is. Nice model. Room
Enough along the handle for
An owl to perch. Thanks! You can pour
It on! A little shut-eye's what
I need."

I guess that's what he got.

David McCord

From The Witch of Willowby Wood

There once was a witch of Willowby Wood,
and a weird wild witch was she, with hair that was snarled
and hands that were gnarled, and a kickety, rickety
knee. She could jump, they say,
to the moon and back, but this I never did see.

Rowena Bennett

Instant Storm

One day in Thrift-Rite Supermart
My jaw dropped with wonder.
For there, right next to frozen peas,
Sat frozen French-fried thunder,
Vanilla-flavored lightning bolts,
Fresh-frozen raindrop rattle—
So I bought the stuff and hauled it home
And grabbed my copper kettle.

I'd cook me a mess of homemade storm!
But when it started melting,
The thunder shook my kitchen sink,
The ice-cold rain kept pelting,
Eight lightning bolts bounced round the room
And snapped my pancake turners—
What a blooming shame!
        Then a rainbow came
And spanned my two front burners.

X. J. Kennedy

Kangaroo and Kiwi

A crazy kangaroo I knew
Who'd always giggle ("Tee-hee!")
Grabbed a big flat pie and let it fly
At a little peewee kiwi.

That kiwi, though, she ducked down low
And let that missile miss her.
It circled back and it landed—whack!—
In the kangaroo's own kisser.

Said kiwi, "My, that's tricky pie,
Must be a custard boomerang?"
"No," said kangaroo, smacking her lips,
"It's lemon kangaroo-meringue."

X. J. Kennedy

About the Teeth of Sharks

The thing about a shark is—teeth,
One row above, one row beneath.

Now take a close look. Do you find
It has another row behind?

Still closer—here, I'll hold your hat:
Has it a third row behind that?

Now look in and . . . Look out! Oh my,
I'll *never* know now! Well, goodbye.

John Ciardi

There Was an Old Woman Named Piper

There was an Old Woman named Piper
Who spoke like a windshield wiper.
   She would say: "Dumb Gump!
   Wet Stump! Wet Stump!"
And then like the voice of disaster
Her words would come faster and faster:
   "Dumb Gump! Dumb Gump!
   Wet Stump! Wet Stump!
   Wet Stump! Wet Stump!
Tiddledy-diddledy-diddledy-bump . . .
      Bump . . .
        Bump . . .
        Bump . . .
          BUMP!"
—Which greatly annoyed Mr. Piper!

William Jay Smith

Look at That!

Look at that!
Ghosts lined up
at the laundromat,
all around the
block.

Each has
bleach
and some
detergent.

Each one seems to
think it
urgent

to take a spin
in a
washing machine

before the
clock
strikes
Halloween!

Lilian Moore

11

The Concert

I left my chambers to attend
A concert by Iturbi
With nothing on but yellow spats,
A wrist watch and a derby.

Arriving early in the hall,
I entered with my house key
And chatted for a moment with
Debussy and Tschaikowsky.

I somersaulted past the guards
And hurried to the wicket . . .
A man obsequiously bowed
And handed me a ticket.

A diamond-studded usherette
Came swinging up to meet me;
I kissed her lightly on the cheek,
Requesting her to seat me.

The opening number filled me with
A most ecstatic feeling . . .
I floated lightly off my chair
And zoomed across the ceiling.

Encouraged by the loud applause
Of audience and musicians,
I tried a graceful loop-the-loop
Between the intermissions.

The news had spread across the town
And thousands were arriving . . .
I took off from the balcony
And did some power diving.

Iturbi grabbed me by the hand
And gave me an ovation . . .
I raised three tubas in the air
And flew them in formation.

A spotlight beamed me to the stage,
I landed down the middle
And finished my performance with
A handspring on a fiddle.

The crowds were milling through the aisles
And everyone was roaring . . .
I pulled the blankets to my neck
And presently was snoring.

Joseph S. Newman

The Bogeyman

In the desolate depths of a perilous place
the bogeyman lurks, with a snarl on his face.
Never dare, never dare to approach his dark lair
for he's waiting . . . just waiting . . . to get you.

He skulks in the shadows, relentless and wild
in his search for a tender, delectable child.
With his steely sharp claws and his slavering jaws
oh, he's waiting . . . just waiting . . . to get you.

Many have entered his dreary domain
but not even one has been heard from again.
They no doubt made a feast for the butchering beast
and he's waiting . . . just waiting . . . to get you.

In that sulphurous, sunless and sinister place
he'll crumple your bones in his bogey embrace.
Never never go near if you hold your life dear,
for oh! . . . what he'll do . . . when he gets you!

Jack Prelutsky

An Easy Decision

I had finished my dinner
Gone for a walk
It was fine
Out and I started whistling

It wasn't long before

I met a
Man and his wife riding on
A pony with seven
Kids running along beside them

I said hello and

Went on
Pretty soon I met another
Couple
This time with nineteen
Kids and all of them
Riding on
A big smiling hippopotamus

I invited them home.

Kenneth Patchen

Blake Leads a Walk on the Milky Way

He gave silver shoes to the rabbit
and golden gloves to the cat
and emerald boots to the tiger and me
and boots of iron to the rat.

He inquired, "Is everyone ready?
The night is uncommonly cold.
We'll start on our journey as children,
but I fear we will finish it old."

He hurried us to the horizon
where morning and evening meet.
The slippery stars went skipping
under our hapless feet.

"I'm terribly cold," said the rabbit.
"My paws are becoming quite blue,
and what will become of my right thumb
while you admire the view?"

"The stars," said the cat, "are abundant
and falling on every side.
Let them carry us back to our comforts.
Let us take the stars for a ride."

"I shall garland my room," said the tiger,
"with a few of these emerald lights."
"I shall give up sleeping forever," I said.
"I shall never part day from night."

The rat was sullen. He grumbled
he ought to have stayed in his bed.
"What's gathered by fools in heaven
will never endure," he said.

Blake gave silver stars to the rabbit
and golden stars to the cat
and emerald stars to the tiger and me
but a handful of dirt to the rat.

Nancy Willard

Into the Streaming Streets

A Rumble

They roar
Out of the river tunnels
Into the streaming streets,
As strong
As a pride of lions,
As long
As a gaggle of geese.
A rumble of trucks
Streaks through the city.
I'd like to drive one
Towering over taxis,
Diesels smoking!
I'd like to drive one,
Cars pulling over,
Cops waving!
I'd like to streak
Through the city
Part of
A rumble of trucks.

Virginia Schonborg

J's the Jumping Jay-Walker

J's the jumping Jay-walker,
   A sort of human jeep.
He crosses where the lights are red.
   Before he looks, he'll leap!
Then many a wheel
Begins to squeal,
   And many a brake to slam.
He turns your knees to jelly
   And the traffic into jam.

Phyllis McGinley

Electric Bogie

Now I do the moon walk,
Watch my feet,
Heel, toe, backward glide,
Right to the beat.
I'm walking in space, man.
I am the ace, man.

Lillian Morrison

21

The Sidewalk Racer

Skimming
an asphalt sea
I swerve, I curve, I
sway; I speed to whirring
sound an inch above the
ground; I'm the sailor
and the sail; I'm the
driver and the wheel
I'm the one and only
single engine
human auto
mobile.

Lillian Morrison

Just for One Day

Hey, sidewalk pacers
bumper riders
long-legged gliders
stalkers, ledge walkers
roof straddlers
fence jumpers
stompers, trouncers
muggers, sluggers
big burly bouncers
alley runners
stabbers, purse grabbers
hurriers, harriers
scared scurriers
all chased and chasers
please cease for a moment
oh please,
lie down in a heap
and sleep.

Lillian Morrison

Eviction

What I remember about that day
is boxes stacked across the walk
and couch springs curling through the air
and drawers and tables balanced on the curb
and us, hollering
leaping up and around
happy to have a playground;

nothing about the emptied rooms
nothing about the emptied family.

Lucille Clifton

Roll Gently, Old Dump Truck

(may be sung to the tune of "Flow Gently, Sweet Afton")

Roll gently, old dump truck,
Through dark city streets
Piled high with cracked eggshells
And leftover beets.

My Daniel's asleep
But he's dreaming of you.
Disturb not my Daniel
When you're rumbling through.

There's a toaster, a TV,
A split baseball bat,
A child's old dump truck
Whose tires are flat.

But Daniel's toy dump truck
Is shiny and new.
So please do not take it
When you're rumbling through.

Charlotte Pomerantz

The City Dump

City asleep
City asleep
Papers fly at the garbage heap.
Refuse dumped and
The sea gulls reap
Grapefruit rinds
And coffee grinds
And apple peels.
The sea gull reels and
The field mouse steals
In for a bite
At the end of night
Of crusts and crumbs
And pits of plums.
The white eggshells
And the blue-green smells
And the gray gull's cry
And the red dawn sky . . .
City asleep
City asleep
A carnival
On the garbage heap.

Felice Holman

The Bridge

A bridge
by day
is steel and strong.
It carries
giant trucks that roll along
above the waters
of the bay.
A bridge is steel and might—
till night.

A bridge
at night
is spun of light
that someone tossed
across the bay
and someone caught
and pinned down tight—
till day.

Lilian Moore

Frightening!

Here it comes!
   huge bulk
   in the darkness
   the long freighter
   blacker than the water
   silent as a ghostship
   stealing by
   slowly
   down the dark river.

        Claudia Lewis

Manhattan Lullaby

Lulled by rumble, babble, beep,
let these little children sleep;
let these city girls and boys
dream a music in the noise,
hear a tune their city plucks
up from buses, up from trucks
up from engines wailing *fire!*
up ten stories high, and higher,
up from hammers, rivets, drills,
up tall buildings, over sills,
up where city children sleep,
lulled by rumble, babble, beep.

Norma Farber

To
the
Edge
of
the
Dashing
Sea

The Wind Came Running

The Wind came running
over the sand,
it caught and held me
by the hand.

It curled and whirled
and danced with me
down to the edge
of the dashing sea.

We danced together,
the Wind and I,
to the cry of a gull
and a wild sea cry.

Ivy O. Eastwick

The Sea Gull Curves His Wings

The sea gull curves his wings,
the sea gull turns his eyes.
Get down into the water, fish!
(if you are wise.)

The sea gull slants his wings,
the sea gull turns his head.
Get deep into the water, fish!
(or you'll be dead.)

Elizabeth Coatsworth

Wild Day at the Shore

Upward a gull
Outward a tern
Upward and outward and seaward.
Inward the wind
Downward the waves
Inward and downward and leeward.
  Wind, waves, and sky.
  Gull, tern, and I.

Felice Holman

From Sea Songs

Crashing on dark shores, drowning, pounding
breaker swallows breaker. Tide follows
tide. Lost in the midnight witchery
moon watches, cresting tall waves, pushing
through mist and blackness the cold waters.

Myra Cohn Livingston

From The Rime of the Ancient Mariner

Beyond the shadow of the ship,
I watched the water-snakes:
They moved in tracks of shining white,
And when they reared, the elfish light
Fell off in heavy flakes.

Within the shadow of the ship
I watched their rich attire:
Blue, glassy green, and velvet black,
They coiled and swam; and every track
Was a flash of golden fire.

Samuel Taylor Coleridge

Seal

See how he dives
From the rocks with a zoom!
See how he darts
Through his watery room
Past crabs and eels
And green seaweed,
Past fluffs of sandy
Minnow feed!
See how he swims
With a swerve and a twist,
A flip of the flipper,
A flick of the wrist!
Quicksilver-quick,
Softer than spray,
Down he plunges
And sweeps away;
Before you can think,
Before you can utter
Words like "Dill pickle"
Or "Apple butter,"
Back up he swims
Past Sting Ray and Shark,
Out with a zoom,
A whoop, a bark;
Before you can say
Whatever you wish,
He plops at your side
With a mouthful of fish!

William Jay Smith

The Kayak Paddler's Joy at the Weather

When I'm out of the house in the open,
  I feel joy.
When I get out on the sea by chance,
  I feel joy.
If it is really fine weather,
  I feel joy.
If the sky really clears nicely,
  I feel joy.
May it continue thus
  for the good of my sealing!
May it continue thus
  for the good of my hunting!
May it continue thus
  for the good of my singing match!
May it continue thus
  for the good of my drum song!

Ammassalik Eskimo

Old Man Ocean

Old Man Ocean, how do you pound
Smooth glass rough, rough stones round?
   Time and the tide and the wild waves rolling,
   Night and the wind and the long grey dawn.

Old Man Ocean, what do you tell,
What do you sing in the empty shell?
   Fog and storm and the long bell tolling,
   Bones in the deep and the brave men gone.

Russell Hoban

The Sea

To me the sea is a continual miracle,
The fishes that swim—the rocks—the motion of the waves
   —the ships with men in them,
What stranger miracles are there?

Walt Whitman

The
Jet
Stream
Roars
In

Jet Stream

When, like lions bursting forth,
The jet stream roars in from the north
The air grows cold and thunderclaps
Waken children from their naps;
Birds huddle and refuse to fly
And people bend as they go by.

Mary O'Neill

The Wind

I can get through a doorway without any key,
And strip the leaves from the great oak tree.

I can drive storm-clouds and shake tall towers,
Or steal through a garden and not wake the flowers.

Seas I can move and ships I can sink;
I can carry a house-top or the scent of pink.

When I am angry I can rave and riot;
And when I am spent, I lie quiet as quiet.

James Reeves

Windy Nights

Whenever the moon and stars are set,
   Whenever the wind is high,
All night long in the dark and wet,
   A man goes riding by.
Late in the night when the fires are out,
Why does he gallop and gallop about?

Whenever the trees are crying aloud,
   And ships are tossed at sea,
By, on the highway, low and loud,
   By at the gallop goes he.
By at the gallop he goes, and then
By he comes back at the gallop again.

Robert Louis Stevenson

Where Would You Be?

Where would you be on a night like this
With the wind so dark and howling?
Close to the light
Wrapped warm and tight
Or there where the cats are prowling?

Where would you wish you on such a night
When the twisting trees are tossed?
Safe in a chair
In the lamp-lit air
Or out where the moon is lost?

Where would you be when the white waves roar
On the tumbling storm-torn sea?
Tucked inside
Where it's calm and dry
Or searching for stars in the furious sky
Whipped by the whine of the gale's wild cry
Out in the night with me?

Karla Kuskin

Winter Is a Wolf

Winter is a
  drowsy wolf
        full of summer sleep.
        He'll awaken and arise
        when the hunger in his eyes
        grows ravenous and deep.

Winter is a
  clever wolf
        we will see him creep
        down the Wind's way
        sly and slow
        in a suit of fleecy snow
        pretending he's a sheep.

Winter is a
  magic wolf
        no man-made cage can keep.
        Crouching low on padded paws,
        licking his enormous jaws,
        earthward he will leap.

Grace Cornell Tall

The Snowstorm

Ever since Tuesday the snow has been falling
And falling and falling
And falling.
No people are stirring, no car-motors whirring,
No chickadees calling.

The bushes are clouds, and the cars sit like igloos
Deserted on roadsides and slopes.
There's wool on the pines, and the telegraph lines
Are sagging white ropes.

With everything changing its shape and its color
On sidewalk and highway and lawn
Or else disappearing from sight and from hearing
As Friday comes on. . . .

It's easy to dream that the snow will keep snowing
And snowing and snowing
And snowing
For week after week, till there's only the peak
Of the church steeple showing.

Kaye Starbird

Christmas Eve

There is a wonder in the world tonight
That I can feel, as well as hear and see.
The snowflakes cover all the earth with white
And fur my window tree.

High in the sky, I watch the star that led
The shepherds from the hilltop with its gleam.
A distant church-bell chimes; and safe in bed
Expectant children dream.

Outside my room, like little yellow moons,
The street-lights glimmer in a double row,
While strangers, softly humming Christmas tunes,
Lean homeward through the snow.

Kaye Starbird

Rain Song

White floating clouds,
clouds like the plains,
come and water the earth.
Sun, embrace the earth
to make her fruitful.
Moon,
lion of the north,
bear of the west,
badger of the south,
wolf of the east,
shrew of the earth,
speak to the cloud people for us,
so that they may water the earth.

Sia Indians

in Just-spring

in Just-
spring   when the world is mud-
luscious and the little
lame balloonman

whistles   far   and wee

and eddieandbill come
running from marbles and
piracies and it's
spring

when the world is puddle-wonderful

the queer
old balloonman whistles
far   and   wee
and bettyandisbel come dancing

from hop-scotch and jump-rope and
it's
spring
and
   the

      goat-footed
balloonman   whistles
far
and
wee

e. e. cummings

Casting
Their
Nets
for
Stars

The Night Fishermen

When moonbeams ripple across the sky
and the moon is a silver dish,
the night fishermen sail along,
casting their nets for fish.

When the wind is blowing among the stars
and the moon is a drinking horn,
the night fishermen sail the sky,
casting their nets till morn.

The song they sing is a sailor's chant
while the moon rocks in their spars,
and they sail along through the silver night,
casting their nets for stars.

Casting their silver nets they come,
tossed by the moon's bright beams,
the night fishermen sailing along,
casting their nets for dreams.

Phyllis Root

Summer Stars

Bend low again, night of summer stars.
So near you are, sky of summer stars,
So near, a long arm man can pick off stars,
Pick off what he wants in the sky bowl,
So near you are, summer stars,
So near, strumming, strumming,
   So lazy and hum-strumming.

Carl Sandburg

From Counting

Counting the stars
As they glitter bright white
Is lovely indeed
And a marvelous sight
When the air is as fresh
As the first night in fall.
But I always have a feeling
That comes very softly stealing
When my head with stars is reeling
That I didn't count them all.

Karla Kuskin

Stars

The stars are too many to count.
The stars make sixes and sevens.
The stars tell nothing—and everything.
The stars look scattered.
Stars are so far away they never speak
when spoken to.

Carl Sandburg

Winter Moon

How thin and sharp the moon is tonight!
How thin and sharp and ghostly white
Is the slim curved crook of the moon tonight!

Langston Hughes

who knows if the moon's

who knows if the moon's
a balloon, coming out of a keen city
in the sky—filled with pretty people?
(and if you and i should

get into it, if they
should take me and take you into their balloon,
why then
we'd go up higher with all the pretty people

than houses and steeples and clouds:
go sailing
away and away sailing into a keen
city which nobody's ever visited, where

always
       it's
               Spring)and everyone's
in love and flowers pick themselves

e. e. cummings

The Horseman

I heard a horseman
  Ride over the hill;
The moon shone clear,
The night was still;
His helm was silver,
  And pale was he;
And the horse he rode
  Was of ivory.

Walter de la Mare

We Will Watch the Northern Lights

We will watch the Northern Lights
playing their game of ball
in the cold, glistening country.
Then we will sit in beauty on the mountain
and watch the small stars
in their sleepless flight.

*Abanaki Indians
of the Eastern Woodland*

The Rumbly Night Train

I cross the old bridge
In fog and in rain.
I cross the old bridge
On the rumbly night train.

I look for my dream
On the bridge where I found it
And then, alas, lost it
In fog and in rain.

And so I keep crossing
And crossing and crossing
For deep is my longing
To dream it again.

Some night I'll find
My dream on the bridge
And take it with me
On the rumbly night train.

And then I'll cross back,
Holding tight to my dream,
And when I cross over,
I'll dream it again.

Charlotte Pomerantz

How Nice to Be a Speckled Frog

The Frog

How nice to be
        a
        speckled
        frog
with all those
        colors
        in
        a
        bog
AND SIT THERE ALL DAY LONG AND SOG
how nice at noon
to keep so cool
just squatting in your private pool
or when enough of THAT you've had
        to sun
        on
        your own lily pad.

But best of all at rise of moon
with you
and all your friends
in tune
as *jug-o'-rum*
and *jing-a-ring*
and thrilling *peep-peep-peep*
you sing
till
    listening
            we
                fall
                    asleep
                         slowly
            listening
      fall
asleep.

Conrad Aiken

The Snake

A snake slipped through the thin green grass
A silver snake
I watched it pass
It moved like a ribbon
Silent as snow.
I think it smiled
As it passed my toe.

Karla Kuskin

The Hound

It's funny to look at a hurrying hound,
Pursuing a scent that's attractive.
He gallops around
With his nose to the ground
And only the back of him active.

Kaye Starbird

The Porcupine

I watched a weeping porcupine
Come wending through the wildsome wood.
He rested near a mossy patch.
He sniffed and whiffed.
He sadly stood.
With woeful breath
He huffed and puffed,
While I spied smiling there,
And quills and quills
And quills and quills
Shot through the quill-filled air.
He wandered on,
That porcupine,
Loud laughing o'er the hills,
And now 'tis he
Is filled with glee.
'Tis me that's filled with quills.

Karla Kuskin

Hippopotamus

See the handsome hippopotamus,
Wading on the river-bottomus.
He goes everywhere he wishes
In pursuit of little fishes.
Cooks them in his cooking-potamus.
"My," fish say, "he eats a lot-of-us!"

Joanna Cole

The Ballad of Red Fox

Yellow sun yellow
Sun yellow sun,
When, oh, when
Will red fox run?

When the hollow horn shall sound,
When the hunter lifts his gun
And liberates the wicked hound,
Then, oh, then shall red fox run.

Yellow sun yellow
Sun yellow sun,
Where, oh, where
Will red fox run?

Through meadows hot as sulphur,
Through forests cool as clay,
Through hedges crisp as morning
And grasses limp as day.

Yellow sky yellow
Sky yellow sky,
How, oh, how
Will red fox die?

With a bullet in his belly,
A dagger in his eye,
And blood upon his red red brush
Shall red fox die.

Melvin Walker la Follette

Father Wolf's Midnight Song

The East Wind is up
And the jack rabbit flees.
Cast for the scent
That still clings to the trees.

Howl, wolves, and sing to the moon.

The air is our map
And the scent points the way.
Up pack, and out pack,
And follow the prey.

Sing, wolves, for morning comes soon.

The hunt is our dream time
And day is our night.
We slip through the starshine,
We sleep through the light.

Howl, wolves, and sing to the moon.
Sing, wolves, for morning comes soon.

Jane Yolen

Spider

I sing no song, I spin instead.
High on the loft above your head.
I weave my stillnesses of thread.

I loop my wiring silver-clear,
to light your manger chandelier.
Listen! my web is what you hear.

Norma Farber

Wild Ducks

When ducks are crying
in the sky
and calling me
to rise and fly
I wish that I
were winged and wild,
a mallard
who was once a child.

Sandra Liatsos

Canoe and Ducks

In smooth single file
eight mergansers glide;
first in a circle
then in a row they
ride the water mirror.

Now they huddle,
now spread out, now
dip heads in the lake
without a splash;
then rise and shake
their feathers,
following the leader.

We watch the silent
aquacade. They
sail on one by one,
and, dipping paddles,
we glide as soundlessly,
the sun, now
dipping too and gone
below the horizon.

Lillian Morrison

Feathers

Everything that lives
wants to fly,
a Mohawk friend
said to me
one winter afternoon
as we watched
grosbeaks take seeds,
fluttering close
to our eyes.

Those were
dinosaurs once,
he said,
but they
made a bargain.
They gave up
that power
in return for
the Sky.

Joseph Bruchac

Someone
Small
but
a
Piece
of
It
All

Who Am I?

The trees ask me,
And the sky,
And the sea asks me
> *Who am I?*

The grass asks me,
And the sand,
And the rocks ask me
> *Who I am.*

The wind tells me
At nightfall,
And the rain tells me
> *Someone small.*

> Someone small
> Someone small
> *But a piece*
> > *of*
> > *it*
> > *all.*

> *Felice Holman*

For Poets

Stay beautiful
but don't stay down underground too long
Don't turn into a mole
or a worm
or a root
or a stone

Come on out into the sunlight
Breathe in trees
Knock out mountains
Commune with snakes
& be the very hero of birds

Don't forget to poke your head up
& blink
Think
Walk all around
Swim upstream

Don't forget to fly

Al Young

To Satch

Sometimes I feel like I will *never* stop
Just go on forever
Till one fine mornin'
I'm gonna reach up and grab me a handfulla stars
Swing out my long lean leg
And whip three hot strikes burnin' down the heavens
And look over at God and say
How about that!

Samuel Allen

Dream Variations

To fling my arms wide
In some place of the sun,
To whirl and to dance
Till the white day is done.
Then rest at cool evening
Beneath a tall tree
While night comes on gently,
 Dark like me—
That is my dream!

To fling my arms wide
In the face of the sun,
Dance! Whirl! Whirl!
Till the quick day is done.
Rest at pale evening . . .
A tall, slim tree . . .
Night coming tenderly
 Black like me.

Langston Hughes

From Multi-Colored Balloon

With my multi-colored balloon
I feel just like I'm under a rainbow;
A blue-green and yellow, red-raspberry jello-y
Funderful rainbow.

I can leap in the air like a silly Pooh Bear,
Or a cow jumping over the moon.
When I'm high in the air
I can spy over there
Where the dish ran away with the spoon.

I can play a squeaky old tune on my colored balloon
If I dare to,
Or dress up like a circus-y clown
With a smile or a frown
Anytime that I care to.

Herbert D. Greggs

This Bridge

This bridge will only take you halfway there
To those mysterious lands you long to see:
Through gypsy camps and swirling Arab fairs
And moonlit woods where unicorns run free.
So come and walk awhile with me and share
The twisting trails and wondrous worlds I've known.
But this bridge will only take you halfway there—
The last few steps you'll have to take alone.

Shel Silverstein

Index of Authors and Titles

Index of First Lines

Acknowledgments

"We will watch the Northern Lights . . ." song of the Abanaki Indians of the Eastern Woodlands: From SONGS OF THE DREAM PEOPLE edited by James Houston. Copyright © 1977. Published by Atheneum. Reprinted by permission of James Houston.

"The Frog" by Conrad Aiken: Reprinted with permission of Atheneum Publishers, an imprint of Macmillan Publishing Company, from CATS AND BATS AND THINGS WITH WINGS by Conrad Aiken. Copyright © 1965 by Conrad Aiken.

"To Satch" by Samuel Allen: From THE POETRY OF BLACK AMERICA edited by Arnold Adoff (Harper, 1973). Copyright © Samuel Allen. Reprinted by permission of Samuel Allen.

"The Kayak Paddler's Joy at the Weather" by Ammassalik Eskimo: From I BREATHE A NEW SONG, POEMS OF THE ESKIMO edited by Richard Lewis. Copyright © 1971 by Richard Lewis. Reprinted by permission of Richard Lewis.

"The Witch of Willowby Wood" by Rowena Bennett: Copyright © 1966 by Rowena Bennett. Reprinted by permission of Kenneth C. Bennett.

"Feathers" by Joseph Bruchac: From *Cricket* Magazine. Reprinted by permission of the author.

"About the Teeth of Sharks" by John Ciardi: From YOU READ TO ME, I'LL READ TO YOU by John Ciardi. (Lippincott) Copyright © 1962 by Curtis Publishing Co.

"Eviction" by Lucille Clifton: From GOOD TIMES by Lucille Clifton. Copyright © 1969 by Lucille Clifton. Reprinted by permission of Curtis Brown, Ltd.

"The Sea Gull Curves His Wings" by Elizabeth Coatsworth: Reprinted with permission of Macmillan Publishing Company from SUMMER GREEN by Elizabeth Coatsworth. Copyright 1947 by Macmillan Publishing Company, renewed 1975 by Elizabeth Coatsworth Beston.

"Hippopotamus" by Joanna Cole: Copyright © 1984 by Joanna Cole, from A NEW TREASURY OF CHILDREN'S POETRY. Reprinted by permission of Doubleday, a division of Bantam Doubleday Dell Publishing Group, Inc.

"in Just-spring" and "who knows if the moon's" by e. e. cummings. Reprinted from TULIPS & CHIMNEYS by e. e. cummings, Edited by George James Firmage, by permission of Liveright Publishing Corporation. Copyright 1923, 1925 and renewed 1951, 1953 by e. e. cummings. Copyright © 1973, 1976 by the Trustees for the e. e. cummings Trust. Copyright © 1973, 1976 by George James Firmage. Published in the United Kingdom and Commonwealth by Grafton Books, A Division of the Collins Publishing Group. Reprinted by permission of Grafton Books, A Division of the Collins Publishing Group.

"The Horseman" by Walter de la Mare: Reprinted by permission of The Literary Trustees of Walter de la Mare and The Society of Authors as their representatives.

"The Wind Came Running" by Ivy O. Eastwick: From I RODE THE BLACK HORSE FAR AWAY by Ivy O. Eastwick. Copyright renewal © 1988 by Hooper & Woolen, Solicitors of the Estate of Ivy O. Eastwick. Used by permission of Abingdon Press.

"Manhattan Lullaby" by Norma Farber: Copyright © Norma Farber. Reprinted by permission of Thomas Farber.

"Spider" by Norma Farber: From *Cricket* Magazine. Copyright © 1976 by Thomas Farber. Reprinted by permission of Thomas Farber.

Excerpt from "Multi-Colored Balloon" by Herbert D. Greggs: From THE MAGIC OF BLACK POETRY by Raoul Abdul (Dodd, Mead 1972). Reprinted by permission of Dodd, Mead & Company.

"Old Man Ocean" by Russell Hoban: From THE PEDALING MAN by Russell Hoban. Copyright © 1968 by Russell Hoban. Reprinted by permission of Harold Ober Associates Incorporated.

"The City Dump," "Who Am I?," and "Wild Day at the Shore" by Felice Holman: From AT THE TOP OF MY VOICE AND OTHER POEMS by Felice Holman. Copyright © 1970 by Felice Holman. Reprinted by permission of Felice Holman.

About the Anthologist

NANCY LARRICK—teacher, writer, lecturer, and editor—has become a driving force in converting today's children into poetry buffs. She has compiled twenty anthologies of poetry for young people, all with the help of the children themselves. Seven of her anthologies have become mass market paperbacks, and many have been listed as ALA Notable Books.

For a number of years she directed the Poetry Workshop at Lehigh University, where parents and teachers experimented with ways of introducing children and poetry happily.

Today millions of parents know Nancy Larrick as the author of *A Parent's Guide to Children's Reading,* first published in 1958. The book is in its fifth completely revised edition and has sold over a million and a quarter copies.

Nancy Larrick grew up in Winchester, Virginia, graduated from Goucher College, received her master's degree from Columbia University and her doctorate from New York University. She was one of the founders of the International Reading Association and its second president. Today she is home again—in Winchester—where she continues her editorial career with frequent trips for lectures and poetry workshops.

About the Illustrator

CATHARINE O'NEILL was born in Toronto, Ontario, Canada, and received her B.A. from the University of Toronto and an M.S. degree from Cornell University. She is both a children's book illustrator and a cartoonist, and has written and illustrated witty and highly original books of her own. She lives in Ithaca, New York.

84